Jordan
Travel Guide

The Ultimate Travel Guide to Exploring the Best Part Of Jordan

Adam Anise

Table of Contents

CHAPTER 1

Brief History of Jordan

Jordan, officially known as the Hashemite Kingdom of Jordan, is a country located in the Middle East, on the east bank of the Jordan River. It is bordered by Saudi Arabia to the south, Iraq to the northeast, Syria to the north, and Israel and Palestine to the west.

The history of Jordan can be traced back to ancient times. The region has been inhabited by various civilizations, including the Amorites, Moabites, and Edomites, as well as the ancient kingdoms of Israel and Judah. The area was also part of the empires of the Assyrians, Babylonians, Persians, and Greeks, and later the Romans and the Byzantine Empire.

During the 7th century AD, the Arab Islamic empire conquered the region and brought Islam to the area. Jordan became part of the Islamic empire, and the Arab tribes began to settle there.

In the early 20th century, the region of Jordan was part of the Ottoman Empire, but after World War I, the League of Nations granted Britain control of the region as a mandate. In 1946, Jordan became an independent country under the rule of King Abdullah I.

Jordan has played an important role in the Arab-Israeli conflict, signing a peace treaty with Israel in 1994 and becoming one of only two Arab countries (the other being Egypt) to have formal diplomatic relations with Israel.

Throughout the later 20th century and into the 21st century, Jordan has continued to be an important player in the Middle East. The country has played host to a large number of Palestinian and Iraqi refugees and has been active in various peacekeeping efforts in the region. The country also has been successful in developing a vibrant tourism industry, it is now considered a safe destination for visitors from all over the world.

Jordan has also been a relatively stable country in a region plagued by conflict and turmoil, and its monarchy has remained a constant source of stability and continuity throughout the country's history.

Top 10 Attractions in Jordan

Jordan is a country located in the Middle East that is known for its historical and cultural sites, as well as its natural beauty. Some of the top attractions in Jordan include:

Petra

This ancient city is located in modern-day Jordan that is well known for its rock-cut structure. The city was established around the 6th century BCE and was the capital of the Nabataean Kingdom. This city is one of the New Seven Wonders of the World and UNESCO World Heritage Site. The city was built into the side of a mountain and many of the structures, including the Treasury, the Monastery, and the Royal Tombs, were carved directly into the rock. Petra's water conduit system, which brought water to the city from a distant spring, was also impressive and allowed the city to thrive in the desert.

Petra was rediscovered in 1812 by Swiss explorer Johann Ludwig Burckhardt, and since then it has become a major tourist destination. Visitors can explore the ancient city on foot, by horse-drawn carriage, or by camel. Guided tours are also available and provide more detailed information about the history and significance of the various structures. Visitors can also hike to the top of a nearby mountain for a panoramic view of the entire site.

Petra can be visited as a day trip from Amman, Jordan's capital city, or spend more time in Petra to discover and explore more. Tourists also can find many activities and tours to do around Petra and nearby areas.

In addition to the ancient architecture, Petra is also known for its stunning natural scenery. The city is surrounded by towering cliffs and canyons, and there are several hiking trails that allow visitors to explore the surrounding area. One popular trail is the hike to the Monastery, a large rock-cut structure that is similar in design to the Treasury but larger in scale. The trail to the Monastery is steep and strenuous, but it offers incredible views of the surrounding landscape.

Another popular trail is the one to the High Place of Sacrifice, which is an ancient altar located at the top of a nearby mountain. This trail is also steep, but it provides a more strenuous workout and an even more spectacular view of the city.

Also, Visitors can take a hot air balloon ride over Petra to view the ancient city from above and enjoy the surrounding landscape.

Petra is open all year round, but the best time to visit is from October to April when temperatures are cooler and more comfortable for sightseeing. June through September can be hot in Petra.

Visitors to Petra should also be prepared for the heat and should wear comfortable shoes and bring plenty of water. Sunscreen and a hat are also highly recommended.

5 best places to stay in Petra

Petra Marriott Hotel: This luxurious hotel is located in the heart of Petra, offering breathtaking views of the ancient city. The hotel features an outdoor swimming pool, a spa, and several on-site dining options.

Movenpick Resort Petra: This modern resort is located just a short walk from the main entrance to Petra, offering easy access to the ancient city's main sites. The resort features an outdoor pool, spa, and fitness center, as well as several on-site dining options.

Petra Guesthouse: This budget-friendly guesthouse offers simple accommodations and a convenient location near the main entrance to Petra. It is a good option for visitors looking to explore Petra on a budget.

Petra Palace Hotel: This hotel is located just outside Petra's main entrance, offering easy access to the ancient city. The hotel features an outdoor pool and a restaurant on-site, as well as views of the surrounding mountains.

Little Petra Bedouin Camp: This unique accommodation option allows visitors to experience

Petra in a more authentic way, by staying in a traditional Bedouin camp on the edge of the ancient city.

The camp offers basic accommodations and a chance to immerse yourself in the local culture and customs.

It's advisable to book your accommodation well in advance.

Wadi Rum

This desert valley is located in southern Jordan. It is known for its unique red-orange sandstone mountains and otherworldly landscapes, which have made it a popular destination for tourists.

Activities in Wadi Rum include hiking, camel trekking, 4WD tours, and rock climbing. Visitors can also take a hot air balloon ride or a scenic flight to get a bird's-eye view of the valley. Some tour operators also offer overnight camping trips in traditional Bedouin tents, where tourists can experience the local culture and customs.

The area is also popular for its film and TV locations. Wadi Rum was used as a filming location for the movie Lawrence of Arabia, and more recently it was the set for movies such as The Martian and Star Wars: Rogue One.

The local Bedouin people have a long history of living in the desert, and many continue to live a semi-nomadic lifestyle. Visitors to Wadi Rum may have the opportunity to meet and interact with local Bedouin people, who often offer tours and other services to tourists.

It's worth noting that the Wadi Rum desert is not only a place for entertainment but also holds cultural, historical, and religious importance. Many of the mountains and rock formations hold carvings and inscriptions dating back to the Nabateans and Early Islamic period.

In addition to this, Wadi Rum is a protected area, and visitors are asked to follow certain guidelines to help preserve the natural environment, such as not littering, not driving off road, and not disturbing the wildlife or native plants.

Wadi Rum is a place of great natural beauty, and it is often referred to as the "Valley of the Moon" because of its otherworldly landscapes. The valley is characterized by its red sandstone mountains, sand dunes, and rock formations. There are also several wadis (dry riverbeds) that run through the valley, which can be a great spot for hiking and exploring.

One of the main attractions in Wadi Rum is the Seven Pillars of Wisdom, a group of seven large rock formations that are named after the book of the same name by T.E. Lawrence (Lawrence of Arabia). The rock formations offer great views of the valley and are a popular spot for tourists to take pictures.

There are also several ancient rock inscriptions and carvings in Wadi Rum. The most famous of these is the "Thamudic Inscriptions", located at the entrance of Wadi Rum village. These inscriptions, dating back to Nabatean and Islamic times, are an important archaeological site and a significant glimpse into the history and culture of the area.

The Bedouin people have a deep connection to the desert and its culture. They have been living in Wadi Rum for centuries and continue to do so today. Many Bedouin people offer a variety of services to tourists, including camel trekking, 4WD tours, and camping trips in traditional Bedouin tents.

Visitors to Wadi Rum can also experience Bedouin culture through traditional music and dance performances, which are often arranged for tourists. These performances give a glimpse into the Bedouin lifestyle and their deep connection to the desert.

Overall, Wadi Rum is an incredibly unique and beautiful destination that offers a wide range of activities for visitors to enjoy. Whether you're looking for adventure or relaxation, this desert valley is sure to provide an unforgettable experience.

Best 5 places to stay in Wadi Rum
Wadi Rum Night Luxury Camp: This luxury camp offers traditional Bedouin tents with modern amenities, including private bathrooms and hot showers. The camp also has a restaurant and bar and offers activities such as camel and jeep tours.

Desert Rose Camp: This eco-friendly camp offers traditional Bedouin tents, as well as a dining area and campfire. The camp is powered by solar energy and offers activities such as hiking and camel treks.

Captains Desert Camp: This camp offers traditional Bedouin tents and a central dining area. The camp also offers activities such as jeep and camel tours and is known for its friendly staff.

Bedouin Lifestyle Camp: This traditional camp offers Bedouin tents with private bathrooms and a central dining area. The camp offers activities such as camel treks and star-gazing.

Wadi Rum Bedouin Village Camp: This camp offers traditional Bedouin tents and a central dining area. The camp also has a pool and offers activities such as jeep and camel tours, as well as a traditional Bedouin dinner and show.

Please note that these are just some of the many camps and accommodations available in Wadi Rum, and the best option for you will depend on your individual preferences and needs. Keep in mind that availability, prices, and reviews may change from time to time.

Jerash

Jerash is an ancient Roman city located in present-day Jordan. It is considered one of the best-preserved Roman cities in the Near East and is a popular tourist destination. The city was founded in the 4th century BC and was later conquered by the Romans in 63 BC. During the Roman period, Jerash flourished as a major city in the Decapolis, a league of Ten Roman Cities in the region.

The main attraction in Jerash is the well-preserved Roman city, which includes a hippodrome, a triumphal arch, a theater, public baths, and a variety of temples and plazas. The highlight of the site is the Oval Plaza, which is surrounded by a colonnaded street and features a grand temple at one end. Another notable feature of Jerash is the South Theater, which could seat up to 3,000 people and is still used for performances today.

In addition to the Roman ruins, Jerash also has a number of other historical sites and monuments, including the Temple of Artemis, the Jerash Archaeological Museum, and the Hadrian Arch.

Nowadays, Jerash holds many events every summer which you can enjoy as well like the Jerash Festival of Culture and Arts which features music, dance, and theater performances, traditional crafts, and food.

Jerash is located about 48 kilometers (30 miles) north of the capital city of Amman and can be easily visited as a day trip from Amman or as part of a larger tour of Jordan.

Jerash also offers a variety of other activities for visitors. The city has several parks and gardens, such as the Jerash Citadel Park, which offers views of the surrounding countryside and the ancient city. Visitors can also take a horse-drawn carriage ride through the old city or enjoy shopping at the Jerash

Souk, which sells a variety of traditional Jordanian crafts and souvenirs.

Jerash is also home to a number of modern amenities, including hotels, restaurants, and coffee shops. Visitors can choose from a range of accommodations, from budget-friendly options to luxury resorts. The city also has several tour operators that offer guided tours of the ancient city and other nearby sites.

Overall, Jerash is a must-see destination for anyone interested in Roman history or architecture. The well-preserved ruins provide a unique opportunity to step back in time and experience what life was like in a Roman city nearly 2,000 years ago. And it's also a great destination to discover traditional Jordan, culture, and arts.

5 Best places to stay in Jerash
Jerash Hills Hotel: A 3-star hotel with a great view of the surrounding hills and archaeological sites. It offers comfortable rooms, a restaurant, and an outdoor swimming pool.

Ruins Wall Hotel & Hostel

The Blue House Gerasa

The Olive Branch Hotel

Hadrian's Arch

The Dead Sea

The Dead Sea, also known as the Salt Sea, is a salt lake located in the Jordan Rift Valley between Israel and Jordan. It is the lowest point on Earth, with an elevation of more than 400 meters (1,300 feet) below sea level. The Dead Sea is known for its high salt content, which makes it extremely difficult for fish and other aquatic life to survive in its waters.

The high salt content of the Dead Sea also makes it a popular destination for people seeking the therapeutic benefits of its mineral-rich waters. Visitors to the Dead Sea can float in the water, which is denser than in any other body of water in the world, due to the high salt content. The mineral-rich mud found along the shores of the Dead Sea is also used as a treatment for a variety of skin conditions, including psoriasis and eczema.

Additionally, The Dead Sea has several famous spots such as:
-Ein Gedi Nature Reserve: is a beautiful oasis near the Dead Sea featuring freshwater pools, waterfalls, and hiking trails.

-Masada: is an ancient fortress located on a plateau overlooking the Dead Sea. It was the site of a famous siege by the Romans in the first century CE.

-Qumran: is an archaeological site located along the northwest shore of the Dead Sea, where the Dead Sea Scrolls were discovered in the 1940s.

The Dead Sea has a dry and hot climate, with temperatures often exceeding 40 °C (104 °F) in the summer and it is recommended to visit in the early morning or evening. Also, sunscreen is a must as the UV rays are intense.

In addition to the natural and historical attractions, the Dead Sea area is also home to several luxury resorts, spas, and wellness centers where visitors can enjoy a variety of treatments and services, including mineral baths, mud treatments, massages, and skin care treatments.

The Dead Sea region is also known for its cosmetics and health products that are made from the minerals and mud found in the area. These products are believed to have anti-aging and healing properties and are popular with tourists as souvenirs and gifts.

The Dead Sea is also an important source of minerals, such as potash and bromine, which are used in a variety of industrial and agricultural applications. In recent years, the extraction of minerals from the Dead Sea has been a major source of income for the countries that border the lake, such as Israel and Jordan.

It is important to note that the water level of the Dead Sea has been receding in recent years, due to a combination of factors including reduced water supply from the Jordan River, mineral extraction, and changing climatic conditions. Conservation efforts are ongoing in an attempt to preserve the unique ecosystem of the Dead Sea.

In summary, the Dead Sea is a unique destination that offers visitors an opportunity to experience the beauty of nature, the history of ancient civilization, the therapeutic benefits of mineral-rich waters and mud, and the luxury of spa and wellness services. It is a must-visit spot for tourists looking for one of a kind experience.

Best 5 places to stay near the Dead Sea
The Kempinski Hotel Ishtar Dead Sea: Located on the shores of the Dead Sea, this luxury hotel offers stunning views of the sea and the surrounding mountains. It features a variety of rooms and suites, as well as a range of on-site amenities including several outdoor pools, a spa, and a private beach.

The Mövenpick Resort & Spa Dead Sea: This 5-star resort is located on the northeastern shore of the Dead Sea and offers a range of room types and suites, as well as an on-site spa and private beach.

The Dead Sea Marriott Resort & Spa: This 5-star resort is located on the southern shore of the Dead Sea and offers a range of room types and suites, as well as an on-site spa, private beach, and several dining options.

The Crowne Plaza Dead Sea: This 4-star hotel is located on the northeastern shore of the Dead Sea and offers a range of room types and suites, as well as an on-site spa, private beach, and several dining options.

The Holiday Inn Resort Dead Sea: This 4-star resort is located on the southern shore of the Dead Sea and offers a range of room types and suites, as well as an on-site spa, private beach, and several dining options.

It is worth mentioning that all of the hotels mentioned are quite luxurious and would be a good choice for those looking for a spa experience or for those who want to relax and enjoy the benefits of the Dead Sea.

Aqaba

Aqaba is a port city located in the far south of Jordan, on the Gulf of Aqaba. It is the only coastal city in Jordan and is an important destination for tourists visiting the country. Aqaba is known for its warm climate, beaches, and coral reefs, making it a popular destination for water sports such as diving and snorkeling. The city is also home to a number of historical and cultural sites, including the Aqaba Fort, the Aqaba Museum, and the Aqaba Archaeological Museum.

Additionally, Aqaba is a popular entry point for visitors looking to explore the nearby desert and natural reserves such as Wadi Rum, Petra, and the

Dead Sea, some of the most important tourist attractions in Jordan.

The city is also known for its excellent seafood and traditional Bedouin cuisine, as well as its vibrant nightlife. Aqaba is served by the King Hussein International Airport, and there are also regular bus and taxi services connecting the city to other parts of Jordan.

Aqaba is a unique city with a rich history and culture, and there are many different things to see and do. One of the most popular tourist activities is snorkeling and diving in the Gulf of Aqaba. The clear waters of the gulf are home to a wide variety of marine life, including over 1,000 species of fish, as well as coral reefs and shipwrecks.

The city is also home to several historical and cultural sites, including the Aqaba Fort, which dates back to the late 1800s and was used to defend the city during World War I. The fort now serves as a museum and offers a glimpse into the city's past.

Another notable historical site in Aqaba is the Aqaba Archaeological Museum, which features a collection of artifacts and ancient relics from the region, including pottery, sculpture, and inscriptions from the Nabatean and Roman periods.

For those interested in outdoor activities, Aqaba offers a variety of options, including hiking and camel trekking in the nearby desert. The Wadi Rum, Petra is located around 200 KM from Aqaba. And the Dead Sea.

Aqaba is a great destination for those looking for a mix of history, culture, and outdoor activities, as well as a taste of the traditional Bedouin lifestyle.

Best 5 places to stay in Aqaba
InterContinental Aqaba Resort: This luxurious resort is located on the beach and offers a variety of amenities, including multiple swimming pools, a spa, and several dining options.

DoubleTree by Hilton Aqaba: This hotel is located in the city center and offers a rooftop pool, a fitness center, and several dining options.

Al Manara, a Luxury Collection Hotel, Aqaba: This 5-star hotel features a private beach, an outdoor pool, a spa, and several dining options.

Aqaba Gulf Hotel: This 4-star hotel is located on the beach and offers a swimming pool, a spa, and a restaurant.

Mövenpick Resort & Residence Aqaba: Located on the beachfront, this resort features multiple swimming pools, a spa, and several dining options.

Please note that the above list is not a ranking, but just a list of a few places that you may consider while choosing to stay in Aqaba, Jordan. There are lots of other available choices as well. Depending on what you are looking for you may need to do more research for your preferences.

Amman Citadel

The Amman Citadel, also known as Jabal al-Qal'a, is an ancient historical site located in the heart of Amman, Jordan. The citadel sits atop a hill in the center of the city and offers panoramic views of the surrounding area. The site has been continuously inhabited since the Bronze Age and has been ruled by various cultures and empires over the centuries, including the Roman, Byzantine, and Islamic periods.

The most notable remains at the Amman Citadel are the ruins of the Temple of Hercules, which dates back to the Roman period, and the Umayyad Palace, which was built during the 8th century AD.

There is also a Byzantine church and an Ottoman-era mosque on the site. The citadel also includes an archaeological museum displaying artifacts from the various cultures and periods that have inhabited the site.

Visiting the Amman Citadel is a popular tourist activity and is open to visitors every day except Friday. The site is accessible by car and on foot, and there is a parking lot available at the base of the hill. Visitors can walk or take a shuttle bus to the top of the hill. Guides are also available to provide a more in-depth tour of the site.

The site is considered by many as a cultural and historically important site in Jordan and the Middle East, it also gives an insight into how the city evolved and was inhabited by various civilizations.

Amman Citadel is also a great spot to take in the beauty of the city. The hilltop location provides panoramic views of the surrounding area, including the old city and the modern downtown. Visitors can also see the Roman Theater, which is located just below the citadel and can seat up to 6,000 people. The theater is still in use today and is the site of various cultural and musical events.

There are also several restaurants and cafes nearby the site, which provide a great spot to relax and enjoy the views after touring the citadel. Visitors can also walk around the old city, which is located just below the citadel and is home to many traditional shops and markets.

The site is a great place to explore and learn about the history of the city, visitors who are interested in archaeology, history, and culture can find a lot to discover and learn.

It is worth noting that, The site is relatively well-preserved, it has been excavated and conserved in recent years, however, some areas are still covered in sand, making it hard to see the details of the buildings.

Best 5 places to stay in Amman Citadel
Four Seasons Hotel Amman: This 5-star hotel is located in the heart of Amman, offering spectacular views of the city and the Citadel. The hotel features luxurious guest rooms and suites, a fitness center, and a rooftop pool.

InterContinental Amman: This 5-star hotel is located in the Abdali district, a short drive from the Citadel. The hotel features elegantly appointed guest rooms and suites, a fitness center, and a rooftop pool with views of the city.

Le Royal Hotel Amman: This 5-star hotel is located in the Shmeisani district, within easy walking distance of the Citadel. The hotel features spacious guest rooms and suites, a fitness center, and an outdoor pool.

Crowne Plaza Amman: This 4-star hotel is located in the Shmeisani district, a short drive from the Citadel. The hotel features comfortable guest rooms and suites, a fitness center, and an indoor pool.

Al Qasr Metropole Hotel: This 4-star hotel is located in the downtown area of Amman, within easy walking distance of the Citadel. The hotel features comfortable guest rooms and suites, a fitness center, and an outdoor pool.

All of these hotels are located near the Citadel and offer easy access to the historic site and other attractions in Amman. However, prices and amenities can vary, so it is best to check the specific information of the hotel that you are interested in.

Roman Theater in Amman

The Roman Theater in Amman, Jordan is a well-preserved ancient Roman structure that dates back to the 2nd century AD. It is believed to have been built during the reign of Emperor Antoninus Pius. The theater is carved into a hillside and has a seating capacity of around 6,000. The stage area of the theater has a diameter of 34 meters and is surrounded by three levels of stone seating. The theater is a popular tourist attraction in Amman and is often used for cultural performances and events. The theater is open for visits to the public most days of the week, and the entry fees are nominal. It is considered one of the best-preserved ancient Roman theaters in the world.

Visitors can walk around the theater and take in the impressive architectural details and learn about the history of the site from informative displays. It's also a great spot for photography enthusiasts, as the theater provides an incredible backdrop for pictures with an ancient ruin and a modern city in the background.

The Roman Theater complex also includes a number of other ruins and artifacts from the Roman period, such as an Odeon (a smaller theater for musical performances) and a number of cisterns and other structures. The Odeon is located just north of the theater and is smaller in size, but still well-preserved.

The area around the theater has been developed into a park, and visitors can also explore other nearby historical sites, such as the nearby Nymphaeum, which was a monumental fountain in the Roman period, and the Ummayad Palace, which dates back to the 8th century AD and is one of the largest and best-preserved examples of Umayyad architecture in Jordan.

Visiting the Roman Theater in Amman is a great way to learn about the history and culture of the region, and it is a must-see attraction for anyone interested in ancient history and architecture.

Many visitors include it in their itinerary while visiting the city, as it is relatively easy to reach and there are several tour guides available that offer guided tours of the theater and other historical sites in the area.

Best 5 places to stay in Roman Theater

The Four Seasons Hotel Amman: This luxurious hotel is located in the heart of the city, just a short distance from the Roman Theater. It offers guests the highest level of comfort and service, including a fitness center, indoor and outdoor swimming pools, and a spa.

Le Royal Hotel Amman: This elegant hotel is located in the Jabal Amman neighborhood, near the Roman Theater. It offers comfortable rooms and suites, as well as a fitness center, indoor swimming pool, and a spa.

The W Amman: This trendy hotel is located in the Abdali neighborhood, near the Roman Theater. It offers guests a unique and modern experience, with stylish rooms and suites, a fitness center, an indoor swimming pool, and a spa.

The Bristol Hotel: This historic hotel is located in the heart of the city, close to the Roman Theater. It offers guests comfortable rooms and suites, as well as a fitness center, indoor swimming pool, and a spa.

City Citadel Hotel: This budget-friendly hotel is located in the Jabal Amman neighborhood, near. It offers simple, yet comfortable rooms.

Kerak Castle

Kerak Castle is a Crusader castle located in present-day southern Jordan, near the town of Al-Karak. The castle was built in the 12th century by the Lord of Montreal, Humphrey IV, and served as a major stronghold for the Crusaders during the Middle Ages. It is one of the largest Crusader castles in the region and is known for its well-preserved fortifications, including a massive donjon (keep) and a network of towers and walls.

During the 12th century, the castle played an important role in the politics of the Kingdom of Jerusalem, serving as a base for the Knights Hospitaller. It was also the site of several battles, including a major siege in 1183 led by Saladin, the Muslim leader who would eventually retake Jerusalem from the Crusaders.

The castle is part of UNESCO world heritage sites and it's open for visitors from 8 am to 4 pm daily except Friday.

Kerak Castle was first built in the 1140s. Its strategic location at the crossroads of trade routes and its proximity to the Gulf of Aqaba is what made it an important base for the Crusaders in their battles against the Muslim armies of the region. Over the centuries, the castle was expanded and strengthened, and by the 12th century, it was one of the largest and most heavily fortified Crusader castles in the region.

During the 12th century, the castle played a significant role in the politics of the Kingdom of Jerusalem. It was a base for the Knights Hospitaller and was involved in several important battles, including a major siege led by the Muslim leader Saladin in 1183. Saladin was ultimately able to capture the castle, but the Crusaders retook it a few years later.

After the fall of Jerusalem in 1187, Kerak Castle remained one of the last Crusader outposts in the region and continued to play a strategic role in the region's battles until it was eventually captured by the Mamluks in 1291.

After the fall of the crusaders the Castle was used by the Mameluks, Ottoman Empire and in the 20th century was handed to the Hashemite Kingdom of Jordan.

Today, Kerak Castle is a popular tourist destination and historical site. The castle's well-preserved ruins and impressive fortifications provide a glimpse into the history of the Crusader era, and visitors can also explore the castle's halls and towers, including the massive donjon (keep), which was used as a palace by the crusader lords.

There is a visitor center that provides information about the castle, and guided tours of the castle's fortifications and halls are available. Visitors can also enjoy panoramic views of the surrounding area from the castle's towers.

Kerak Castle is a must-see attraction for history buffs, providing an opportunity to explore one of the best-preserved examples of Crusader architecture and gain insight into the complex history of the region.

Best places to stay in Kerak Castle
Beit Al Baraka: This traditional stone house is located in the historic town of Kerak and offers views of the castle. The house has been restored to its original design and features traditional furnishings and decor.

Al-Qasr Hotel: This hotel is located within the walls of Kerak Castle and offers views of the castle and the surrounding area. The hotel features traditional decor and a restaurant.

Tower Castle Hotel: This hotel offers comfortable rooms and a variety of facilities, including a restaurant, terrace, and pool. It is conveniently located near the center of Karak and many of the city's top attractions.

Madaba

Madaba is a city located in central Jordan, known for its rich history and cultural heritage. The city is home to several significant historical and religious sites, including the ancient city of Madaba, which was a thriving city in the Roman and Byzantine periods.

One of the most famous sites in Madaba is the Madaba Map, an ancient mosaic map of the Holy Land, which was discovered in 1884 in the floor of the Saint George's Church. The map, which dates back to the 6th century AD, is considered one of the most important surviving examples of Byzantine art and is a valuable historical resource for understanding the region during that time period.

Another popular site in Madaba is Mount Nebo, a hill located to the northwest of the city, which is mentioned in the Bible as the place where Moses viewed the Promised Land. The site features a basilica and a memorial to Moses, as well as panoramic views of the Jordan Valley and the Dead Sea.

The city also features many other mosaics and churches, including the Church of the Apostles, and the Greek Orthodox Church of St. George. You can also visit a number of souvenir shops and art galleries to buy traditional crafts and souvenirs.

Madaba is also known as a hub for hiking and outdoor activities, as there are many trails leading from Madaba to the surrounding area, with beautiful landscapes, ancient villages, and monasteries to explore.

You can also find several hotels and restaurants in the city center to accommodate visitors, for a pleasant stay.

Madaba is also known for its vibrant cultural scene. The city hosts several annual festivals and events, including the Madaba Festival of Culture and Arts, which features traditional music and dance performances, as well as exhibitions of art and crafts.

Another event is the Madaba Summer Festival, which takes place every summer and features live music performances, traditional dance, and other cultural activities.

Madaba is also a great starting point for day trips to other parts of Jordan. The city is located near the Dead Sea, the city is also located close to the capital of Amman, which is a short drive away, like the Roman Theater, The Citadel, and much more.

Madaba is a city that offers a unique blend of history, culture, and natural beauty, making it a popular destination for tourists visiting Jordan.

Best places to stay in Madaba
The Grand Hotel Madaba: This hotel is located in the center of Madaba and offers comfortable rooms, a restaurant and bar, and a fitness center. It is a great option for those looking for a more luxurious stay in the city.

Madaba hills villa, Dulaylat al Ḥamā'idah
The three-bedroom air-conditioned home has direct access to a terrace with garden views and a kitchenette that is fully furnished.

The Madaba Hotel: This hotel is located in the heart of Madaba, close to many of the city's top attractions such as the St. George's Church and the Madaba Map. It offers comfortable rooms, a restaurant and bar, and a rooftop terrace with views of the city.

Mount Nebo

Mount Nebo is a peak in Jordan, located about 817 meters (2,680 feet) above sea level. It is believed to be the site where Moses was granted a view of the Promised Land by God before he died and was buried in an unknown location in the area. The mountain is located in the vicinity of the city of Madaba and is considered a significant religious site for both Jews and Christians.

A Byzantine church was built on the mountain in the 4th century AD, which was later rebuilt during the Early Islamic period. The church was excavated in the early 20th century and remains of mosaic floors were found inside.

Mount Nebo has been considered a UNESCO World Heritage Site since 2011, in addition to its religious significance, The Mountain is considered an important ecological site for the preservation of the Mediterranean High Mountain and the Eastern Mediterranean shrubland.

Many Christian and Jewish pilgrimage tours include a visit to Mount Nebo as part of their itinerary. The mountain can be accessed by road from Amman or Madaba. There is also a visitor's center at the summit which offers information about the history and significance of the site.

Best places to stay in Mount Nebo
The Jordan Valley Marriott Resort & Spa, located in the city of Madaba, offers luxurious accommodations and is a great option for those looking for a more upscale experience.

The Petra Guesthouse, located in the city of Petra, offers a convenient location for those who want to visit both Mount Nebo and the famous ancient city of Petra.

The Mount Nebo Hotel, located in the town of Madaba, is a great option for those looking to be close to the mountain while still being in a bustling town.

Note: There are many other great places to stay near these places, but the above-mentioned are considered some of the best.

Activities You Can Do From January to December

There are a variety of activities that tourists can enjoy throughout the year, depending on their interests and the time of year they plan to visit. Here are some activities to consider for each month of the year:

January
-The cool temperatures in January make for comfortable exploring of the city's ruins and monuments.

-Take a hot air balloon ride over the desert landscape of Wadi Rum, also known as the Valley of the Moon.

February
-Celebrate the annual Jordan Festival in Amman, which features music, dance, and other cultural performances from around the world.

-Ski or snowboard at the country's only ski resort, the Faraya Mzaar Ski Resort, which is located in the mountains near the Lebanese border.

March

-Visit the desert castle of Azraq, an ancient fortified complex that was built during the Islamic Golden Age.

-Go on a jeep tour of Wadi Rum to see the desert's natural beauty and learn about Bedouin culture.

April

-Visit the ancient Roman city of Jerash, which features well-preserved ruins of temples, theaters, and other structures.

-Take a dip in the Dead Sea, which is known for its high salt content and healing properties.

May

-Attend the Jerash Festival for Culture and Arts, which takes place in the ancient Roman city of Jerash and features music, dance, and other cultural performances.

-Visit the Ajloun Castle, a medieval fortress that was built to protect the region from Crusaders.

June

-Explore the ancient Nabatean city of Petra, which is known for its rock-cut architecture and impressive sculptures.

-Visit the Jordan Museum in Amman, which houses artifacts from Jordan's ancient history, including items from the Petra archaeological site.

July

-Attend the Jerash Festival for Culture and Arts, which takes place in the ancient Roman city of Jerash and features music, dance, and other cultural performances.

-Visit the ruins of the Byzantine-era desert fortress of Qasr al-Hallabat, which is located in the eastern desert.

August

-Take a dip in the Dead Sea, which is known for its high salt content and healing properties.

-Visit the ancient city of Aqaba, Jordan's only coastal city, which is home to a well-preserved medieval fort and a bustling market.

September
-Visit the ancient Nabatean city of Petra, which is known for its rock-cut architecture and impressive sculptures.

-Attend the Petra by Night event, where the ancient city is lit up and can be explored by candlelight.

October
-Take a hike in the Dana Biosphere Reserve, which is home to a variety of wildlife and offers stunning views of the surrounding landscape.

-Visit the ancient city of Jerash, which features well-preserved ruins of temples, theaters, and other structures.

November
-Attend the Petra International Poetry Festival, which takes place in the ancient Nabatean city of Petra and features poets from around the world.

-Visit the Wadi Mujib Nature Reserve, which is home to a variety of plants and animals, as well as a breathtaking gorge that can be explored by raft.

December

-Visit the ancient Nabatean city of Petra, which is known for its rock-cut architecture and impressive sculptures.

-Attend the Christmas Market in Amman, which is a great opportunity to purchase traditional crafts, gifts, and souvenirs as well as try some local food.

-Take a trip to the city of Aqaba, Jordan's only coastal city, which offers a variety of activities such as swimming, snorkeling, diving, windsurfing, and sailing.

-Visit Umm Qais, the ancient city of Gadara, one of the Decapolis cities that offers panoramic views of the Golan Heights, Jordan Valley, and the Sea of Galilee.

Overall Jordan has a lot to offer as a tourist destination and these are just a few examples of the many activities that can be enjoyed throughout the year. Whether you're interested in history, culture, or nature, there is something for everyone to discover in this beautiful country.

CHAPTER 2

Top Jordanian Cuisine to Try Out

Jordanian cuisine is a blend of Mediterranean, Middle Eastern, and Bedouin influences. Some popular dishes and ingredients in Jordanian cuisine include:

Falafel

One popular food in Jordan is falafel, which is a deep-fried ball or patty made from ground chickpeas or fava beans. It is often served on a piece of pita bread with vegetables and tahini sauce. Falafel is a popular street food in Jordan and can be found at many street vendors and restaurants throughout the country.

Another popular way to enjoy falafel in Jordan is by visiting a falafel stand or food truck, where you can watch as the falafel is freshly prepared and deep-fried right in front of you. These stands are usually located in busy areas like markets or near popular tourist attractions and are a great option for a quick and satisfying meal.

Falafel is a must-try for tourists visiting Jordan, it's tasty, affordable, and a staple street food in the country, it can be found in many street vendors and restaurants throughout the country, and it is also a great way to experience the local cuisine.

Baba Ganoush

Baba ganoush is a popular Middle Eastern eggplant dip or spread that is typically made with mashed cooked eggplant, tahini (sesame seed paste), olive oil, lemon juice, and seasonings such as garlic, cumin, and salt. It is commonly served as an appetizer or as a side dish with pita bread, vegetables, or crackers. In Jordan, baba ganoush is often garnished with parsley or paprika and may also include additional ingredients such as yogurt or mint.

In Jordan, baba ganoush is a popular dish that can be found in many restaurants, cafes, and street vendors. It is often served as a mezze, which is a selection of small dishes typically served as appetizers before a main course. Tourists visiting Jordan can try baba ganoush in a traditional setting, such as a local restaurant that serves authentic Jordanian cuisine, or in a more casual setting such as a street food vendor or food truck.

It is also a dish that can be made at home and it is very easy to make. Tourists can also buy some ready-made Baba Ganoush in local supermarkets and grocery stores.

Baba ganoush is also a vegetarian and vegan-friendly dish, making it a great option for those with dietary restrictions. Additionally, it's a healthy dish as it's made of eggplants, which are high in fiber and low in calories.

Baba ganoush is a delicious and traditional Middle Eastern dish that is widely available in Jordan and a great option for tourists looking to try authentic Jordanian cuisine. It's easy to find, easy to make, and a healthy dish that can be enjoyed by everyone.

Shawarma

Shawarma is a popular street food dish in Jordan that is made by grilling meat (usually chicken or lamb) on a spit and then shaving it off to be served in a wrap or pita bread with vegetables and various sauces. It is a delicious and affordable option for tourists to try while visiting Jordan. The shawarma can be found in many street vendors, local restaurants, and even in food courts of malls. It is often served with tahini sauce, garlic sauce, and other sauces, as well as tomatoes, cucumbers, and pickles. Some restaurants also offer a vegetarian version of shawarma, usually made with falafel or eggplant. It is considered a must-try dish for tourists visiting Jordan.

In addition to traditional shawarma, there are also variations of the dish that can be found in Jordan. For example, "shish tawook" is a variation that is made with marinated chicken, and "shawarma Lahm bi ajeen" is a version that is made with a ground meat mixture and served in a pizza-like crust.

Tourists can also find different types of shawarma places, from street vendors to sit-down restaurants, each with its own unique flavors and styles. Some restaurants offer a traditional and authentic experience, while others may have a more modern and upscale atmosphere.

When trying shawarma, it is important to keep in mind that it is typically a very filling and hearty dish, so it may be best to share with a friend or save room for other delicious dishes that Jordan has to offer. Additionally, it's also worth noting that Shawarma is usually considered fast food or street food in Jordan, and it could be a bit greasy, so it's best to be mindful of that if you are health conscious.

Hummus

Jordan is known for its delicious hummus, which is a popular dish made from chickpeas, tahini, lemon juice, and garlic. It is typically served as a dip or spread and is often accompanied by pita bread or vegetables. In Jordan, it is common to find street vendors selling hummus as well as restaurants that specialize in serving it. Tourists visiting Jordan should definitely try the local hummus, as it is considered a staple of the country's cuisine and offers a unique and delicious flavor compared to hummus found in other regions. Additionally, many restaurants in Jordan serve hummus with a variety of toppings such as meat, pine nuts, and spices.

In addition to trying the traditional hummus, tourists in Jordan should also look for variations on the dish, such as hummus with added spices or herbs, or topped with different types of meat or vegetables. Many restaurants also offer "ful medames" which is a variation of hummus that includes whole chickpeas and is often served as a main dish.

It is also worth noting that hummus is often served as part of a larger meze platter, along with other traditional Middle Eastern dishes such as falafel, tabbouleh, and baba ghanoush. These platters are a great way to try a variety of different foods and flavors.

Another popular way to enjoy hummus in Jordan is at a "Hummusiya" which is a small restaurant or café that specializes in hummus. These places often have a casual atmosphere and are great spots to grab a quick bite to eat or to enjoy hummus with friends.

In summary, for tourists visiting Jordan, hummus is a must-try dish that offers a unique and delicious taste of the country's cuisine. Whether you try it traditionally or with variations, at a street vendor or a Hummusiyas, you will find the hummus in Jordan to be a standout dish.

Warak Enab

Warak Enab, also known as stuffed vine leaves, is a traditional Middle Eastern dish made with vine leaves filled with a mixture of rice, herbs, and sometimes meat. It is a popular dish in many countries in the region, including Jordan. For tourists visiting Jordan, trying Warak Enab is a great way to experience local cuisine and culture. The dish is often served as an appetizer or side dish and can be found at many restaurants and street food vendors throughout the country.

In addition to trying Warak Enab at restaurants, tourists can also learn to make the dish themselves by taking a cooking class that focuses on traditional Jordanian cuisine. These classes are a great way to learn more about the ingredients and techniques used to make Warak Enab, as well as other traditional dishes.

Warak Enab is also a very common dish in Mediterranean and Middle Eastern cuisine, and it is a staple in Lebanese, Syrian and Palestinian cuisine as well. It is a healthy dish and is often served cold as part of a mezze platter.

Another way to experience Warak Enab while in Jordan is by visiting local markets and food fairs, where vendors often sell homemade Warak Enab and other traditional dishes. These events offer a great opportunity to sample different variations of the dish and to purchase some to take home as a souvenir.

Overall, Warak Enab is a delicious and traditional dish that offers a taste of the local culture for tourists visiting Jordan. It is a must-try for any food lover.

Fattoush

Fattoush is a popular salad dish in Middle Eastern cuisine that is often served as an appetizer or side dish. The salad typically consists of tomatoes, cucumbers, parsley, mint, and onions, which are all diced and mixed together. The salad is then dressed with lemon juice, olive oil, and sumac, a Middle Eastern spice that has a tangy, lemony flavor. Pita bread is also often added to the salad, which is then broken up and mixed in. Some variations also include lettuce, radishes, and/or feta cheese. It is considered a healthy and delicious dish that is enjoyed by locals and tourists alike.

It is a dish that is commonly found in Middle Eastern restaurants and street vendors. It is a popular dish among tourists visiting Jordan as it is a perfect representation of the local cuisine. Many restaurants and street vendors in Jordan serve Fattoush as a traditional appetizer, as it is a refreshing and light dish that is perfect for a warm climate. The dish is not only delicious but also a healthy option, as it is made from fresh vegetables and herbs, and is low in fat and calories.

It is also quite versatile and can be enjoyed as a main dish or as a side dish. Some variations include adding grilled chicken or lamb for a more substantial meal. Fattoush is usually served cold and is a great dish to enjoy during the summer months.

It is also a great way to experience the local culture and flavors of Jordan. The dish is a great representation of the mix of flavors and ingredients that are found in the Middle East. Many tourists enjoy trying Fattoush while visiting Jordan to get a taste of the local cuisine and culture.

Knafeh

Knafeh is a traditional Middle Eastern dessert made of phyllo dough, cheese, and sweet syrup. It is a popular dish in Jordan and is often served as a breakfast or dessert item. The sweet syrup and cheese give the dish a unique sweetness and creaminess, while the phyllo dough provides a crispy texture. The dish can be found at many local restaurants and street vendors throughout Jordan and is a must-try for tourists visiting the country. It is sometimes spelled as Kanafeh or Knefeh.

In addition to the traditional version, there are also variations of the dish that include different types of cheese or fillings such as nuts or fruit. It can also be made with different types of syrup, such as honey or rosewater.

Jordanian Knafeh is also known for its beautiful presentation and it is usually served on a platter, garnished with crushed pistachios, and drizzled with syrup. It is a very rich and sweet dessert, so it is usually served in small portions.

For those looking to try Knafeh during their visit to Jordan, it can be found in many local bakeries and sweet shops, as well as in some traditional restaurants. Some of the famous places in Jordan to find great Knafeh include Al Quds, Habiba, and Al Khalil.

Jordan Knafeh is a delicious and unique dessert that is definitely worth trying while visiting Jordan. It is a perfect combination of sweet, creamy, and crispy, and it is a true representation of traditional Jordanian cuisine.

Tabbouleh

Tabbouleh, also spelled tabouleh or tabouli, is a traditional Levantine salad made from parsley, tomatoes, onions, and bulgur wheat. It is often seasoned with lemon juice, olive oil, and spices such as mint, cumin, and black pepper. It is a popular dish in Jordan and is often served as a side dish or appetizer. Tabbouleh is a healthy and refreshing option for tourists as it is high in protein, fiber, and vitamins. It is a perfect dish for vegetarians and vegans and can be easily found in most restaurants in Jordan.

In addition to being a popular dish in Jordan, tabbouleh is also a staple in Lebanese, Syrian, and

Palestinian cuisine. The dish is typically served chilled, making it a great option for hot summer days.

Tourists visiting Jordan can try tabbouleh in a variety of settings, from street food vendors to fine dining restaurants. Many restaurants will also offer variations of the traditional recipe, such as adding different types of herbs or vegetables. Some may even use quinoa or couscous instead of bulgur wheat.

Tabbouleh is also a popular dish to take on picnics and outdoor excursions, as it travels well and can be enjoyed cold. It's a great option for those looking for a quick and easy lunch on the go.

Overall, tabbouleh is a must-try dish for tourists visiting Jordan, as it is a delicious and healthy option that represents the local culture and cuisine.

Kebab

Kebab, also known as Kofta, is a popular dish that is often served to tourists. It typically consists of ground meat (usually lamb or beef) mixed with spices and herbs and is grilled or fried. The meat is often served with a variety of sides such as rice, hummus, tabbouleh, and pita bread. It can also be served in a sandwich wrap with vegetables and yogurt sauce. Kebab shops and restaurants are widely available in cities and towns throughout Jordan, making it a convenient and delicious option for tourists looking to try local cuisine.

Jordanian cuisine is a fusion of Mediterranean, Middle Eastern, and Bedouin cultures, and kebab is considered one of the most popular street foods in the country. It is a common food for locals and tourists alike and can be found in many restaurants and street vendors throughout the country.

Tourists visiting Jordan should also try other traditional dishes such as mansaf, the national dish of Jordan, which is made of lamb cooked in a yogurt sauce and served with rice or bread, and the traditional Bedouin dish of Zarb, which is a type of underground barbecue made with meat and vegetables cooked in a pit oven.

Overall, Jordan Kebab is a must-try for tourists visiting the country, it's delicious, affordable, and can be found everywhere.

Mezze

Mezze is a variety of small dishes that are traditionally served as appetizers in Middle Eastern cuisine, particularly in Jordan. These dishes can include a range of options such as dips (such as hummus or tabbouleh), salads, grilled meats, and various pickled vegetables. Mezze is often served as a sharing platter among a group and is a popular option for tourists to try a variety of different flavors and dishes in one meal.

Best time to visit

The best time to visit Jordan largely depends on what you plan to see and do during your trip. If you're interested in exploring Petra, the ancient city carved into the rock, the cooler months of September to November or March to May are the best time to visit. The temperatures are mild and comfortable during these months, making it easier to explore the site. For travelers interested in hiking or visiting Wadi Rum, the best time to visit is from October to April, when temperatures are cooler and more comfortable for outdoor activities. For visitors looking for the warmest weather, the best time to visit is from May to September, but be aware that the temperatures can be extremely hot during this period and may make outdoor activities more challenging.

Additionally, it's worth noting that if you plan to visit Jordan during the months of Ramadan, it's important to be respectful of the local culture and customs. Many businesses and restaurants may be closed during the day, and public consumption of food and drink is not allowed during this time.

Overall, the best time to visit Jordan depends on your personal preferences and what you plan to see and do during your trip. If you're looking for the best weather and comfortable temperatures, September to November and March to May are the best. And if you're interested in experiencing the warmest weather, May to September is the best time to visit, but be aware that temperatures can be extreme during this period.

CHAPTER 3

Jordan Traveling Essentials

Some essential items to consider when traveling to Jordan include:

General Essentials

A valid passport and visa: Make sure your passport is valid for at least six months beyond your planned stay in Jordan. You can obtain a visa upon arrival at the airport in Jordan, or in advance from a Jordanian embassy or consulate.

Comfortable walking shoes: Jordan is home to many historical and cultural sites, such as Petra, that require a lot of walking.

Modest clothing: Jordan is a conservative country, and it's important to dress modestly in order to respect local customs. Women should avoid wearing revealing clothing, and both men and women should avoid shorts or short-sleeved shirts when visiting religious sites.

Sun protection: Jordan can be quite hot, especially during the summer months.

A reusable water bottle: Tap water in Jordan is safe to drink, but it's a good idea to bring a reusable water bottle to refill as needed.

Cash and credit card: Many places in Jordan still do not accept credit cards, so it's a good idea to bring some cash in Jordanian dinars.

Travel insurance: It's always a good idea to have travel insurance in case of any unexpected emergencies or issues during your trip.

Hiking Essentials

When planning a hiking trip to Jordan, there are several essential items that tourists should bring to ensure a safe and enjoyable experience.

Proper Footwear: Hiking boots or sturdy trail shoes with good traction are a must.

Clothing: Dress in layers to accommodate for changing temperatures and bring a waterproof and windproof jacket. Wear long pants to protect against the sun and rocks.

Hydration: Bring a water bottle or hydration system and make sure to drink plenty of water before, during, and after the hike.

Food: Pack snacks and a lunch to fuel your hike. Pack high-energy foods such as nuts, dried fruit, and chocolate.

First Aid Kit: A basic first aid kit should include bandages, gauze, tape, pain relievers, and any personal medications.

Sun Protection: Wear a wide-brimmed hat, and sunglasses and apply sunscreen with a high SPF.

Map and compass: Carry a map and compass, or a GPS device, and know how to use them.

Headlamp or flashlight: Bring a headlamp or flashlight in case of an emergency or if you plan to hike in the early morning or late afternoon.

Emergency whistle: Bring an emergency whistle to signal for help if needed.

Trash bags: Pack out all trash and leave the trails as you found them.

It's also important to be aware of and follow local hiking rules and regulations and to inform someone of your itinerary and expected return time before embarking on your hike.

Snorkeling Essentials

When snorkeling or diving in Jordan, tourists should pack a few essential items to ensure a safe and enjoyable experience. These include:

A snorkel and diving mask: These are necessary for seeing underwater and should fit comfortably and securely.

Fins: Fins will help with propulsion and maneuverability while snorkeling or diving.

Wetsuit or dive skin: A wetsuit or dive skin will provide thermal protection and help to prevent sunburn.

Dive computer or depth gauge: These devices will allow divers to monitor their depth and time underwater, which is important for safety.

Dive light: A dive light can be useful for exploring caves or for night diving.

Dive knife: A dive knife can be used to cut fishing lines or other debris that may be encountered while diving.

Dive flag: A dive flag is an important safety item that should be used to alert boats and other watercraft to the presence of divers in the area.

Sunscreen: Sunscreen is essential to protect the skin from sun damage while snorkeling or diving.

First aid kit: A small first aid kit should be packed in case of minor injuries.

It's also recommended to check the location and weather conditions before the trip and pack accordingly.

Beach Essentials

Some recommended beach packing items for tourists visiting Jordan include:

Sunscreen: The sun can be intense in Jordan, especially during the summer months, so it's important to protect your skin from sunburn and UV damage.

Swimwear: Jordan has several beaches along the Red Sea where tourists can go swimming and snorkeling.

Comfortable footwear: Jordan beaches are rocky and sandy, so comfortable shoes like sandals or water shoes are recommended for exploring the shoreline.

A hat or sunglasses: To protect your face and eyes from the sun.

Light, breathable clothing: Jordan can get hot during the day, so it's important to wear lightweight, loose-fitting clothing that will keep you cool and comfortable.

A beach towel or mat: To sit or lay on while relaxing on the beach.

A reusable water bottle: To stay hydrated while exploring Jordan's beaches.

Snacks and refreshments: Some beaches may not have many food options, so it's a good idea to bring your own snacks and refreshments.

Beach bag: To carry all your items in.

Insect repellent: To protect yourself from insects.

Camera: To capture memories of your beach experience.

Personal hygiene items: You may want to bring items such as a toothbrush, toothpaste, and hand sanitizer to keep yourself clean and refreshed while enjoying the beach.

A change of clothes: After a day at the beach, you'll likely want to change into something dry and clean.

Any necessary medications or first-aid supplies: It's always a good idea to be prepared for any unexpected medical issues.

Cash or credit card: Some beaches may not have ATM machines or card readers, so it's important to have cash on hand to pay for parking, and entrance fees or to buy souvenirs.

Beach games: To have some fun on the beach, you can bring items such as frisbees, beach balls, or beach volleyball.

A good book or a music player: To relax and enjoy the beach.

A beach umbrella or a parasol: To provide shade from the sun.

A beach chair or a portable hammock: To sit comfortably and relax on the beach.

It is always good to check with locals or tour guides about the specific beach you will be visiting in Jordan as some may have different rules or regulations regarding the items that you can bring to the beach.

Traveling Itinerary

Jordan is a country with a rich history and culture, and there are many things to see and do. Here is a sample itinerary for a 7-day & 2 weeks trip to Jordan:

1-week Travel Itinerary

Here is a suggested 1-week itinerary for a trip to Jordan:

Day 1: Arrival in Amman
-Upon arrival in Amman, check into your hotel and take some time to rest and adjust to the time difference.

-In the evening, explore the city and visit the Roman Theater and the Citadel, which offer great views of the city.

Day 2: Amman to Petra
-Take a drive to Petra, which is about a 3-hour drive from Amman.

-Check into your hotel and spend the rest of the day exploring the ancient city.

-Don't miss the Treasury, Monastery, and Royal Tombs.

Day 3: Petra
-Spend a full day exploring Petra, and take a guided tour to make the most of your visit.

-There are many trails to explore, including the High Place of Sacrifice and the Wadi Farasa.

-In the evening, enjoy a traditional Bedouin dinner and catch a Petra by Night tour, where the ancient city is lit up by candlelight.

Day 4: Petra to Wadi Rum
-Take a drive to Wadi Rum and check into your desert camp.

-Spend the afternoon exploring the desert by jeep or camel.

-Watch the sunset over the desert and enjoy dinner under the stars.

Day 5: Wadi Rum to Aqaba
-Take a drive to Aqaba and check into your hotel.

-Spend the day exploring the city and visiting the Aqaba Fort and the Aqaba Archaeological Museum.

-In the evening, take a boat tour to see the Gulf of Aqaba and the Red Sea.

Day 6: Aqaba to the Dead Sea
-Take a drive to the Dead Sea and check into your hotel.

-Spend the day relaxing on the beach and floating in the salty water.

-Don't forget to cover yourself with the mud, it is known for its healing properties.

Day 7: Dead Sea to Amman
-Take a drive back to Amman and spend your last day exploring the city.

-Visit the Jordan Museum or the King Abdullah Mosque.

-In the evening, enjoy a farewell dinner at a traditional restaurant before departing Jordan.

Please Note that this itinerary is a suggestion only, you may adjust the time spent in each place depending on your interest. Also, Jordan offers a lot more than what is discussed here, so you may have to choose the places you would like to visit.

2-week Travel Itinerary

Here is a sample 2-week travel itinerary for Jordan:

Day 1: Arrive in Amman and check-in into your lodging area.

Day 2: Visit the Roman Theater and the Citadel in Amman.

Day 3: Drive to Petra, the ancient Nabatean city, and spend the day exploring the site.

Day 4: Continue exploring Petra and take a hike through the surrounding mountains.

Day 5: Drive to Wadi Rum and take a jeep tour of the desert.

Day 6: Spend a night in a Bedouin camp in Wadi Rum.

Day 7: Drive to Aqaba, Jordan's only coastal city, and spend the day relaxing on the beach.

Day 8: Drive to the Dead Sea and spend the day floating in the salty waters.

Day 9: Visit the ancient city of Jerash.

Day 10: Drive to the Dana Biosphere Reserve and take a hike through the beautiful landscape.

Day 11: Visit the medieval city of Karak and the nearby Crusader castle.

Day 12: Drive to the desert castles of Qasr Amra and Qasr Kharana.

Day 13: Return to Amman and spend the day shopping and exploring the city.

Day 14: Depart from Amman.

Note: Depending on the interest and time availability, the itinerary can be adjusted accordingly. It's always good to have some extra buffer days in case of any unexpected events.

This itinerary provides a great overview of the highlights of the country, but there are many other things to see and do as well. You could also consider visiting the ancient city of Bosra or the mosaics at Madaba. And don't forget to haggle for souvenirs at the local markets.

CHAPTER 4

Jordan On a Budget

Visiting Jordan on a budget is definitely possible and can be a great way to explore the country without breaking the bank. Here are some tips to help you plan your trip:

Accommodation
Look for budget-friendly options such as hostels or guesthouses. These types of accommodations are often more affordable than hotels, and many of them provide great amenities and services.

Transportation
Jordan has a good public transportation system and taking buses or trains can be a cost-effective way to get around. You can also consider car rental, but keep in mind that it can be more expensive than using public transportation.

Food
Jordan is known for its delicious street food and local restaurants. Eating at these types of establishments is often much cheaper than dining at more upscale restaurants.

Sightseeing

Many of Jordan's top tourist attractions, such as Petra and Wadi Rum, have entrance fees. However, by purchasing a Jordan Pass, you can gain access to many of these sites at a discounted rate.

Be flexible

Try to be flexible with your travel plans, as last-minute deals and discounts can often be found.

Travel during off-peak season

Jordan's peak tourist season is from May to September, and prices tend to be higher during this time. If possible, consider traveling during the off-peak season when prices are generally lower.

Plan ahead

Research and plan ahead for your trip to Jordan. This will help you to find the best deals on flights, accommodations, and activities. Websites like Skyscanner and Booking.com allow you to compare prices and find the best deals.

Avoid tourist traps

Jordan is full of tourist traps that can add unnecessary expenses to your trip. Be sure to do your research and avoid places that are known for overcharging tourists.

Stay in budget-friendly areas
Consider staying in budget-friendly areas such as Amman, the capital city, or Aqaba, a coastal city. These areas offer a wide range of affordable accommodation options and are well-connected to other parts of the country.

Be mindful of your spending
Keep track of your spending throughout your trip and stick to your budget. This will help you to avoid overspending and ensure that you have enough money to enjoy your trip to the fullest.

Look for free activities
Jordan has a lot of free or low-cost activities to enjoy, such as visiting local markets and small villages, hiking, and visiting historical sites. The city of Amman, for example, has several Roman ruins and museums, like the Amman Citadel, that you can visit for free.

Use local transportation
Using local transportation like service taxis (shared taxis) is a great way to save money. They are

cheaper than private taxis, and they run frequently
on fixed routes.

Consider a tour package
If you're looking to save money, consider a tour
package that includes accommodation,
transportation, and activities. This can often be
more cost-effective than booking everything
separately.

Bargain
Bargaining is a norm in Jordan, so don't be afraid to
negotiate prices when shopping at markets or
souqs.

Be mindful of tips
Tipping is expected in Jordan, so be prepared to tip
your guide, driver, or hotel staff, but you can always
negotiate the amount if you can't afford it.

The country is a great destination for budget
travelers, with a rich culture, history, and natural
beauty. With a bit of planning, flexibility, and being
mindful of your spending, you can experience all
that Jordan has to offer without breaking the bank.

Getting Around Jordan

Jordan has a well-developed transportation system, making it easy to get around the country. The most popular modes of transportation include buses, taxis, and rental cars.

Buses
The bus system in Jordan is efficient and affordable. There are several bus companies that operate throughout the country, with routes connecting major cities and tourist destinations. Bus tickets can be purchased at the station or on the bus.

Taxis
Taxis are widely available in Jordan and can be hailed on the street or found at designated taxi stands. They are a convenient way to get around, but it is important to negotiate the fare before starting the trip.

Rental Cars
Renting a car in Jordan is a great option for those who want more flexibility in their travels. Drivers must have a valid driver's license and be over 21

years old. It's also important to note that traffic drives on the right side of the road in Jordan.

Trains
Jordan has a limited train service that connects the capital Amman with the northern city of Irbid and the southern city of Ma'an.

Private Tours
Private tours are a great option for those who want a more personalized experience. These can be arranged through tour operators or hotels.

Camels and horses
In Petra and Wadi Rum, you can take a tour on a camel or horseback.

Overall, the most important thing when getting around Jordan is to plan ahead, be aware of your surroundings, and be prepared for unexpected delays.

CHAPTER 5

Tourist Safety Tips

Jordan is generally considered a safe destination for tourists, but it is always important to be aware of potential safety risks and take appropriate precautions.

Political stability

Jordan is a relatively stable country, but political tensions in the region can affect security. Visitors should stay informed about the situation and avoid any large gatherings or protests.

Terrorism

While terrorist attacks are rare in Jordan, they have occurred in the past and could happen again. Visitors should be vigilant and avoid crowded areas.

Crime

Crime rates in Jordan are low, but visitors should still take standard precautions such as keeping valuables safe and avoiding walking alone in unfamiliar areas at night.

Road safety

Driving in Jordan can be hazardous due to poor road conditions and reckless driving. Visitors should be aware of the risks and consider hiring a driver or taking public transportation.

Hot weather

Jordan can be quite hot, especially in the summer months. Visitors should stay hydrated and take appropriate precautions to avoid heat stroke.

Religious and cultural sensitivity

Jordan is a predominantly Muslim country and visitors should be respectful of local customs and traditions. Dress modestly when visiting religious sites and avoid public displays of affection.

Petra

Petra is a popular tourist destination in Jordan and it's important to be aware of the risks involved in visiting the site. Tourists should wear appropriate footwear as the site can be slippery, and also be aware of the heat as temperatures can be quite high.

Dead Sea

The Dead Sea is a popular tourist destination in Jordan, but visitors should be aware of the risks involved in swimming in the sea. The water is extremely salty and can cause skin irritation, and the shore can be slippery and rocky. Visitors should also be aware that the water can be quite warm and there is a risk of sunburn.

Vaccinations
Visitors to Jordan should be up to date on their routine vaccinations and may also consider getting vaccinations for Hepatitis A, Hepatitis B, Rabies, and Meningitis.

Health concerns
Visitors should be aware of the potential health risks in Jordan, including heat stroke, sunburn, and dehydration. They should also be aware of the risk of illnesses such as dengue fever and the West Nile virus, which are transmitted by mosquitoes.

Travel insurance
Visitors are strongly encouraged to purchase travel insurance before traveling to Jordan to protect themselves in case of an emergency.

Emergency services
In case of an emergency, visitors can contact the local authorities by dialing 112 or 911. The U.S. Embassy in Amman is located at: Amman, Al-

Umawyeen St., Abdoun, P.O. Box 354, Amman 11118, Jordan, and the emergency number is +962-6-590-6000

In conclusion, Jordan is a safe destination for tourists but visitors should take standard safety precautions and stay informed about the situation in the country. And also be aware of the specific risks at the main tourist destinations and take the necessary precautions.

Things To Do In Case of Emergency

In case of an emergency in Jordan, there are several things that you should do:

-Contact the local emergency services by dialing 112. This number will connect you to the police, fire department, and ambulance services.

-If you are in the capital city of Amman, the US Embassy can be reached at +(962) (6) 590-6000. The Embassy is open 24 hours a day and can provide assistance in case of an emergency.

-If you are in a remote area and unable to reach emergency services, contact the local authorities or the nearest police station for assistance.

-If you are in a medical emergency, there are several hospitals in Jordan that provide quality medical care. The Jordan University Hospital in Amman is one of the best in the country and is equipped to handle a wide range of medical emergencies.

-If you are involved in a car accident, it is important to call the police and emergency services immediately. The police will investigate the accident and provide assistance to those involved.

-If you are a victim of a crime, contact the police as soon as possible. The police will take a report and provide assistance in getting medical attention if needed.

-In case of a natural disaster like an earthquake, try to stay calm and follow the instructions provided by local authorities. If you are in a building, try to get to a safe place as quickly as possible.

-It is important to be aware of your surroundings and stay informed of any potential hazards or emergency situations that may arise. Being prepared and knowing what to do in case of an emergency can help keep you and your loved ones safe.

-If you are traveling outside of major cities, it is a good idea to carry a personal emergency kit with you, including items such as a first aid kit, water, and non-perishable food.

-If you are a foreign national and become a victim of a crime or other emergency, contact your embassy or consulate for assistance. They can provide you with information on local resources, as well as help you contact family and friends back home.

-It is also a good idea to register with your embassy or consulate when you arrive in Jordan so that they can contact you in case of an emergency.

-If you are planning on traveling to a specific area, it is important to research and be aware of any potential safety or security risks and take appropriate precautions.

In summary, in case of an emergency in Jordan, it is important to contact local emergency services, seek medical attention if needed, and follow the instructions of local authorities. Being prepared and familiarizing yourself with emergency resources and evacuation plans can help keep you and your loved ones safe.

CHAPTER 6

Festival and Events in Jordan

Amman, the capital of Jordan, is one of the world's oldest cities and has existed since antiquity. The nation has seen several different centuries and has been ruled by numerous separate empires. This leads to a wide range of historical, cultural, and religious diversity. Each year, Jordan hosts a number of interesting and notable festivals. The top seven festivals in Jordan are listed below.

Traditional Arts Festival in Aqaba

This Traditional Arts Festival is held in Aqaba, a town in the north of Jordan, a country with a unique culture. This event celebrates the Bedouin culture, which involves showcasing their artistic abilities.

The most alluring feature of Aqaba is that it is the only port city in Jordan. Scuba diving at Tala Bay Beach Resort is well-known around the nation. It is strongly encouraged not to miss any Aqaba Festival events. Diverse diving activities are available to attendees throughout the festival. While giving guests complete freedom, this celebration never fails to amaze them. Usually, visitors to Jordan have low expectations and are pleasantly surprised when they arrive. This festival's spirit embodies the aforementioned rich Arabic heritage and culture.

Celebration month is February
The celebration location is Aqaba

International Theater Festival in Amman

There are several unique events and festivals held in Amman. Whether it's Mother's Day or Valentine's Day, Amman celebrates festivals every day. In a manner similar to other festivals, Jordanians sell their own homemade handicrafts. Additionally, following the popularity of the first year, this city will host the International Dates Festival for a second time. The best and healthiest dates in the world are available for consumption.

This theatrical performance has earned a permanent position in Jordan's traditional and cultural heritage. This is acknowledged as a dependable platform for prospective artists to express themselves and trade creative ideas with the best theatrical gurus in the Arab globe. The free exchange of thoughts and speech continues to enhance the creative environment in Amman.

Celebration month is March
The celebration location is Amman

Azraq Festival

Azraq, a little Jordanian community that serves as the entrance to the Eastern Desert, is hosting a festival of music, dancing, and mouthwatering regional food. The Azraq Festival is one of Jordan's smallest, yet despite its modest size, it consistently draws sizable audiences because of its lively atmosphere. It was created to showcase the community's high-quality art and crafts as well as discuss local customs.

The promotion and display of this magnificent town's culture, art, and crafts is its primary objective. With street dances and music, local cuisine for sale, and a great community gathering, it's a bright and joyous celebration. Even though it's one of Jordan's smallest events, it's worthwhile to witness.

Celebration month is February
The celebration location is Azraq

Muharram

This celebration marks the start of the Islamic New Year and is one of the most well-known holidays in Jordan. After the first month of the Islamic calendar, it is named "Muharram." It takes place every year at a different time on the Gregorian calendar. This is because each new month in the lunar-based Islamic calendar begins with the sighting of the new moon.

The main focus of the celebrations on this day is the birth of Muhammad, the prophet who is responsible for popularizing and establishing Islam in Muslim nations. Muslims go to their mosques to observe it and offer several prayers to Allah each day. Although the exact day changes every year, it is commemorated in all Islamic nations. In many Jordanian towns and cities, Muharram is observed with food, dances, and customs.

The celebration month is June
Celebration location is throughout the nation

Muslim Holidays

Islamic holidays are deeply ingrained in Jordanian culture as a result of the country's predominance of

Muslims. Ramadan and the two Eid celebrations are well-known Islamic "holidays."

Muslim New Year is celebrated on the first day of the Islamic calendar, which commemorates the travel of the prophet Muhammad from Mecca to Medina. Despite the fact that Friday is not a very holy day, all mosques are open, and worship music may be heard all day long.

Celebration month is July
Celebration location is throughout the nation

Festival of Arts and Culture in Jerash

The historic city of Jerash hosts one of the biggest and most well-known festivals not just there but all throughout the nation. Queen Noor Al Hussein started the event in 1981. It has since developed into a global cultural phenomenon. There, guests, artists, and performers from all over the world assemble for a once-in-a-lifetime occasion.

The Jerash Festival typically takes place around the end of July or at the start of August. The summer months are also a relatively sluggish time for tourists due to the heat. Over the course of a week, people can view many genres of art. This event will feature a wide variety of musicians, dancers, vocalists, folklore ensembles, orchestras, ballet, theater, poetry, handicrafts, and other creative demonstrations. The categorization and separation of the performances allow visitors to wander around the runic ambiance of the city.

Celebration month is July to August
The celebration location is throughout the entire nation.

Jordanian Rally

Jordan celebrates its annual Rally every October. The most well-known event in Jordan ended with this one. It is a well-known Jordanian event that attracts guests from all across the nation and beyond. For thrill-seekers and adrenaline junkies, the Rally of Jordan is the ideal rallying and racing event. The construction of a complete race car set draws huge audiences from all around Jordan and the surrounding regions to see this exciting and adrenaline-pumping automotive event and festival.

It takes place in the desert, where the sand dunes are used as driving lanes. With 1008 kilometers of course for rally racers to compete on, it is a beautiful event. You won't want to miss the Jordan Rally if you like cars and racing.

Celebration month is October
The celebration location is Rumman Hill

In Jordan, there is an abundance of festivals, events, and entertainment options that will make your trip a dream come true. Include these seven most well-known events in your Jordan travel itinerary so you may take part completely.

Conclusion

Experience the beauty and adventure of Jordan on your vacation! From the historic city of Petra to the stunning desert landscapes of Wadi Rum, there's something for everyone to enjoy. Take a dip in the Dead Sea, the lowest point on Earth, and discover the ancient history of the Nabatean people. Relax in the luxurious resorts in Aqaba, Jordan's only coastal city, and explore the vibrant underwater world of the Red Sea. Whether you're a history buff, an adventure seeker, or just looking for a relaxing getaway, Jordan has it all.

In Jordan, you'll have the opportunity to explore some of the most unique and beautiful landscapes in the world. The rugged terrain of Petra is home to ancient temples and tombs carved into the rock, and the Wadi Rum desert is a playground for outdoor enthusiasts, offering activities such as camel trekking, rock climbing, and stargazing.

The country's rich cultural heritage is also on full display, with the impressive Roman city of Jerash and the historic city of Amman, both offering a glimpse into the past.

Jordan's unique location also offers the opportunity to visit the biblical sites of Bethany Beyond the Jordan and Mount Nebo, where Moses is said to have viewed the Promised Land.

After a day of exploring, unwind in one of Jordan's luxurious resorts and spas, or indulge in the local cuisine, which blends Mediterranean, Middle Eastern, and Bedouin influences.

Book your Jordan vacation and discover why it's a destination that has something for everyone. Don't miss out on the chance to experience the beauty, history, and culture of this amazing country.

Made in United States
Troutdale, OR
08/15/2023

12099740R00066